The Best Mediterranean Dash Diet Cookbook

A Collection of Delicious Mediterranean Dash Diet Recipes for Your Daily Meals

Kathyrn Solano

Table of contents

GREAT MEDITERRANEAN DIET RECIPES

Kidney Bean, Veggie, And Grape Salad With Feta

Servings:4

Cooking Time: 25 Minutes

Ingredients:

1½ cups red grapes, halved

1 (15-ounce) can red kidney beans, drained and rinsed

10 ounces cherry tomatoes, halved (quartered if tomatoes are large)

4 (6-inch) Persian cucumbers, quartered vertically and chopped

½ cup green pumpkin seeds (pepitas)

½ cup feta cheese

2½ ounces baby spinach leaves (about 4 cups)

½ cup Dijon Red Wine Vinaigrette

Directions:

Place the grapes, kidney beans, cherry tomatoes, cucumbers, pumpkin seeds, and feta in a large mixing bowl and mix to combine.

Place cups of the salad mixture in each of 4 containers. Then place 1 cup of spinach leaves on top of each salad. Pour 2 tablespoons of vinaigrette into each of 4 sauce containers. Refrigerate all the containers.

STORAGE: Store covered containers in the refrigerator for up to 5 days.

Nutrition Info: Total calories: 5; Total fat: 25g; Saturated fat: 6g; Sodium: 435mg; Carbohydrates: 37g; Fiber: 10g; Protein: 16g

Tuna, Kale Slaw, Edamame, And Strawberry Salad

Servings: 3

Cooking Time: 15 Minutes

Ingredients:

2 (5-ounce) cans light tuna packed in water

8 tablespoons Honey-Lemon Vinaigrette, divided

3 cups prepackaged kale-and-cabbage slaw

1 cup shelled frozen edamame, thawed

2 Persian cucumbers, quartered vertically and chopped

1¼ cups sliced strawberries

3 tablespoons chopped fresh dill

Directions:

Place the tuna in a small bowl and mix with 2 tablespoons of vinaigrette.

In a large mixing bowl, place the slaw, edamame, cucumbers, strawberries, and dill. Toss to combine.

Place ⅓ cup of tuna in each of containers. Place one third of the salad on top of the tuna in each container to lessen the chance of the salad getting soggy. Spoon 2 tablespoons of the remaining vinaigrette into each of 3 separate sauce containers.

STORAGE: Store covered containers in the refrigerator for up to days.

Nutrition Info: Total calories: 317; Total fat: 18g; Saturated fat: 2g; Sodium: 414mg; Carbohydrates: 22g; Fiber: 9g; Protein: 22g

Avocado Green Goddess Dip With Veggie Dippers

Servings: 4

Cooking Time: 10 Minutes

Ingredients:

½ teaspoon chopped garlic

1 cup packed fresh parsley leaves

½ cup fresh mint leaves

¼ cup fresh tarragon leaves

¼ teaspoon plus ⅛ teaspoon kosher salt

¼ cup freshly squeezed lemon juice

¼ cup extra-virgin olive oil

½ cup water

1 medium avocado

1 (1-pound) bag baby carrots

2 heads endive, leaves separated

Directions:

Place the garlic, parsley, mint, tarragon, salt, lemon juice, oil, water, and avocado in a blender and blend until smooth.

Place 4 ounces of carrots and half a head of endive leaves in each of 4 containers. Spoon ¼ cup of dip into each of 4 sauce containers.

STORAGE: Store covered containers in the refrigerator for up to 5 days.

Nutrition Info: Total calories: 301; Total fat: 21g; Saturated fat: 2g; Sodium: 373mg; Carbohydrates: 2; Fiber: 13g; Protein: 23g

Cocoa-almond Bliss Bites

Servings: 10

Cooking Time: 1 Hour

Ingredients:

1 medium ripe banana, mashed

3 tablespoons ground flaxseed

½ cup rolled oats

½ cup plain, unsalted almond butter

2 tablespoons unsweetened cocoa powder

¼ cup almond meal

¼ teaspoon ground cinnamon

2 teaspoons pure maple syrup

Directions:

Combine all the ingredients in a medium mixing bowl.

Roll the mixture into 10 balls, slightly smaller than a golf ball, and place on a plate.

Freeze the bites for 1 hour to harden.

Place 2 bites in each of 5 small containers or resealable bags and store in the refrigerator.

STORAGE: Store covered containers or resealable bags in the refrigerator for up to days. If you want to make a big batch, the bites can be frozen for up to 3 months.

Nutrition Info: Per Serving (2 bites): Total calories: 130; Total fat: 9g; Saturated fat: 1g; Sodium: 1mg; Carbohydrates: 11g; Fiber: 3g; Protein: 5g

Tofu And Vegetable Provençal

Servings: 4

Cooking Time: 30 Minutes

Ingredients:

1 pound super-firm tofu, cut into ¾-inch cubes

2 tablespoons freshly squeezed lemon juice

2 tablespoons olive oil

1 teaspoon garlic powder

1 teaspoon herbes de Provence

¼ teaspoon kosher salt

4 teaspoons olive oil, divided

1 (14-ounce) eggplant, cubed into 1-inch pieces (5 to 6 cups)

1 small yellow onion, chopped (about 2 cups)

2 teaspoons chopped garlic

10 ounces cherry tomatoes, halved if tomatoes are fairly large

1 (14-ounce) can artichoke hearts, drained

1 teaspoon herbes de Provence

¼ teaspoon kosher salt

½ cup dry white wine, such as sauvignon blanc

⅓ cup pitted kalamata olives, roughly chopped

1 (½-ounce) package fresh basil, chopped

Directions:

TO MAKE THE TOFU

Place the tofu in a container with the lemon juice, oil, garlic powder, herbes de Provence, and salt. Allow to marinate for 1 hour.

When you're ready to cook the tofu, preheat the oven to 400°F and line a sheet pan with a silicone baking mat or parchment paper. Lift the tofu out of the marinade and place it on the sheet pan. Bake for minutes, flipping the tofu over after 15 minutes. Cool, then place about ½ cup of tofu cubes in each of 4 containers.

TO MAKE THE VEGETABLE RAGOUT

While the tofu is marinating, heat 2 teaspoons of oil in a 12-inch skillet over medium-high heat. When the oil is shimmering, add the eggplant and cook for 4 minutes, stirring occasionally. Remove the eggplant and place on a plate.

Add the remaining 2 teaspoons of oil to the pan, and add the onion and garlic. Cook for 2 minutes. Add the tomatoes and cook for 5 more minutes. Add the eggplant, artichokes, herbes de Provence, salt, and wine. Cover the pan, lower the heat, and simmer for 20 minutes.

Turn the heat off and stir in the olives and basil.

Spoon about 1½ cups of vegetables into each of the 4 tofu containers.

STORAGE: Store covered containers in the refrigerator for up to 5 days.

Nutrition Info: Total calories: 362; Total fat: 17g; Saturated fat: 3g; Sodium: 728mg; Carbohydrates: 32g; Fiber: 9g; Protein: 23g

Cheesy Bread

Servings: 12

Cooking Time: 15 Minutes

Ingredients:

3 cups shredded cheddar cheese

1 cup mayonnaise

1 1-ounce pack dry ranch dressing mix

1 2-ounce can chopped black olives, drained

4 green onions, sliced

2 French baguettes, cut into ½ inch slices

Directions:

Preheat oven to 350 degrees Fahrenheit.

In a medium-sized bowl, combine cheese, ranch dressing mix, mayonnaise, onions, and olives.

Increase mayo if you want a juicier mixture.

Spread cheese mixture on top of your French baguette slices.

Arrange the slices in a single layer on a large baking sheet.

Bake for about 15 minutes until the cheese is bubbly and browning.

Cool and chill.

Serve warm!

Nutrition Info: Calories: 2, Total Fat: 17 g, Saturated Fat: 7.2 g, Cholesterol: 35 mg, Sodium: 578 mg, Total Carbohydrate: 23.9 g, Dietary Fiber: 1.1 g, Total Sugars: 2.4 g, Protein: 11.1 g, Vitamin D: 3 mcg, Calcium: 229 mg, Iron: 2 mg, Potassium: 85 mg

Turkey Meatballs With Tomato Sauce And Roasted Spaghetti Squash

Servings: 3

Cooking Time: 35 Minutes

Ingredients:

FOR THE SPAGHETTI SQUASH

3 pounds spaghetti squash

1 teaspoon olive oil

¼ teaspoon kosher salt

FOR THE MEATBALLS

½ pound lean ground turkey

4 ounces mushrooms, finely chopped (about 1½ cups)

2 tablespoons onion powder

1 tablespoon garlic powder

1 teaspoon dried Italian herbs

⅛ teaspoon kosher salt

1 large egg

FOR THE SAUCE

1 (28-ounce) can crushed tomatoes

1 cup shredded carrots

1 teaspoon garlic powder

1 teaspoon onion powder

¼ teaspoon kosher salt

Directions:

TO MAKE THE SPAGHETTI SQUASH

Preheat the oven to 4°F and place a silicone baking mat or parchment paper on a sheet pan.

Using a heavy, sharp knife, cut the ends off the spaghetti squash. Stand the squash upright and cut down the middle. Scrape out the seeds and stringy flesh with a spoon and discard.

Rub the oil on the cut sides of the squash and sprinkle with the salt. Lay the squash cut-side down on the baking sheet. Roast for 30 to 35 minutes, until the flesh is tender when poked with a sharp knife.

When the squash is cool enough to handle, scrape the flesh out with a fork and place about 1 cup in each of 3 containers.

TO MAKE THE MEATBALLS AND SAUCE

Place all the ingredients for the meatballs in a large bowl. Mix with your hands until all the ingredients are combined.

Place all the sauce ingredients in an by-11-inch glass or ceramic baking dish, and stir to combine.

Form 12 golf-ball-size meatballs and place each directly in the baking dish of tomato sauce.

Place the baking dish in the oven and bake for 25 minutes. Cool.

Place 4 meatballs and 1 cup of sauce in each of the 3 squash containers.

STORAGE: Store covered containers in the refrigerator for up to 5 days.

Nutrition Info: Total calories: 406; Total fat: ; Saturated fat: 5g; Sodium: 1,296mg; Carbohydrates: 45g; Fiber: 10g; Protein: 29g

Salmon Cakes With Steamed Green Bean Gremolata

Servings: 4

Cooking Time: 6 Minutes

Ingredients:

2 (6-ounce) cans skinless, boneless salmon, drained

½ teaspoon garlic powder

⅓ cup minced shallot

2 tablespoons Dijon mustard

2 eggs

½ cup panko bread crumbs

1 tablespoon capers, chopped

1 cup chopped parsley

⅓ cup chopped sun-dried tomatoes

1 tablespoon freshly squeezed lemon juice

1 tablespoon olive oil

Zest of 2 lemons (about 2 tablespoons when zested
with a Microplane)

¼ cup minced parsley

1 teaspoon minced garlic

¼ teaspoon kosher salt

1 teaspoon olive oil

1 pound green beans, trimmed

Directions:

TO MAKE THE SALMON CAKES

In a large bowl, place the salmon, garlic, shallot, mustard, eggs, bread crumbs, capers, parsley, tomatoes, and lemon juice. Stir well to combine.

Form 8 patties and place them on a plate.

Heat the oil in a 12-inch skillet over medium-high heat. Once the oil is hot, add the patties. Cook for 3 minutes on each side, or until each side is browned.

Place 2 cooled salmon cakes in each of 4 containers.

TO MAKE THE GREEN BEANS

In a small bowl, combine the lemon zest, parsley, garlic, salt, and oil.

Bring about ¼ to ½ inch of water to a boil in a soup pot, Dutch oven, or skillet.

Once the water is boiling, add the green beans, cover, and set a timer for 3 minutes. The green beans should be crisp-tender.

Drain the green beans and transfer to a large bowl. Add the gremolata (lemon zest mixture) and toss to combine.

Divide the green beans among the 4 salmon cake containers. If using, place ¼ cup of Garlic Yogurt Sauce in each of 4 sauce containers. Refrigerate.

STORAGE: Store covered containers in the refrigerator for up to 5 days. Uncooked patties can be frozen for 3 to 4 months.

Nutrition Info: Total calories: 268; Total fat: 9g; Saturated fat: 2g; Sodium: 638mg; Carbohydrates: 21g; Fiber: 6g; Protein: 27g

Cherry, Vanilla, And Almond Overnight Oats

Servings: 5

Cooking Time: 10 Minutes

Ingredients:

1⅔ cups rolled oats

3⅓ cups unsweetened vanilla almond milk

5 tablespoons plain, unsalted almond butter

2 teaspoons vanilla extract

1 tablespoon plus 2 teaspoons pure maple syrup

3 tablespoons chia seeds

½ cup plus 2 tablespoons sliced almonds

1⅔ cups frozen sweet cherries

Directions:

In a large bowl, mix the oats, almond milk, almond butter, vanilla, maple syrup, and chia seeds until well combined.

Spoon ¾ cup of the oat mixture into each of 5 containers.

Top each serving with 2 tablespoons of almonds and ⅓ cup of cherries.

STORAGE: Store covered containers in the refrigerator for up to 5 days. Overnight oats can be eaten cold or warmed up in the microwave.

Nutrition Info: Total calories: 373; Total fat: 20g; Saturated fat: 1g; Sodium: 121mg; Carbohydrates: 40g; Fiber: 11g; Protein: 13g

Egg Caprese breakfast cups

Preparation time: 12 minutes

Cooking time: 17 minutes

Servings: 12

Ingredients:

1/2 tsp garlic powder

4 tbsp basil sliced

12 mozzarella balls

3 cups spinach

12 large eggs

1.25 cups chopped tomatoes

1/2 tsp black pepper

3/4 tsp salt

1-2 tbsp Parmesan cheese grated

balsamic vinegar as required

Directions: In greased muffin cups, make a layer of spinach at the bottom.

Arrange tomatoes, mozzarella, and basil above the spinach layer.

In a mixing bowl, mix salt, cheese, black pepper, garlic powder, and eggs.

Add the egg/cheese mixture in layered muffin cups.

Place the muffin cups for 20 minutes in a preheated oven at 350 degrees.

Drizzle balsamic vinegar and serve.

Nutrition Info: Calories: 141 kcal Fat: 10 g Protein: 11 g Carbs: 1 g Fiber: 1.8 g

Asparagus and mushroom frittata with goat cheese

Preparation time: 2 minutes

Cooking time: 8 minutes

Servings: 4

Ingredients:

2 tbsp goat cheese

Two eggs

1pinch of kosher salt

1 tsp of milk

1 tbsp butter

Five trimmed asparagus spears

Three sliced brown mushrooms

1 tbsp chopped green onion

Directions: In a pan, cook mushrooms over medium flame for about three minutes.

Stir in asparagus and cook for two more minutes.

In a bowl, add one tsp of water, eggs, and salt and mix well.

Add the egg mixture to the mushroom mixture, followed by a drizzling of goat cheese and green onions.

Let them cook well until the egg mixture is properly formed.

Shift the pan to the preheated oven and bake for three minutes.

Drizzle cheese and serve.

Nutrition Info: Calories: 331 kcal Fat: 26 g Protein: 20 g Carbs: 7 g Fiber: 2 g

Outrageous herbaceous Mediterranean chickpea salad

Preparation time: 20 minutes

Cooking time: 20 minutes

Servings: 4

Ingredients:

1/2 cup chopped celery with leaves

30 oz chickpeas

1.5 cups chopped parsley

1/2 cup chopped onion

3 tbsp olive oil

3 tbsp lemon juice

Two minced cloves garlic

1/2 tsp kosher salt

One chopped red bell pepper

1/2 tsp black pepper

Directions:

Combine bell pepper, onion, chickpeas, celery, and parsley in a mixing bowl.

In another bowl. Mix olive oil, garlic, salt, lemon juice, and pepper.

Pour olive oil mixture over chickpeas mixture and mix well and serve.

Nutrition Info: Calories: 474 kcal Fat: 16 g Protein: 20 g Carbs: 65 g Fiber: 18 g

Mediterranean quinoa salad

Preparation time: 15 minutes

Cooking time: 0 minute

Servings: 4

Ingredients:

1.5 cups dry quinoa

1/2 tsp kosher salt

1/2 cup extra virgin olive oil

1 tbsp balsamic vinegar minced garlic cloves

1/2 tsp minced basil

1/2 tsp crushed thyme

Black pepper to taste cups arugula

15 oz garbanzo

One package salad savors for toppings

Directions:

In a pot, add water, salt, and quinoa. Cook until quinoa is done. Drain and set aside.

Whisk garlic, pepper, thyme, olive oil, salt, basil, and vinegar in a bowl. The dressing is ready. Keep it aside.

In a big sized bowl, combine salad savor content, arugula, quinoa, and beans.

Pour dressing over the arugula mixture and serve after sprinkling basil over it.

Nutrition Info: Calories: 583 kcal Fat: 33 g Protein: 15 g Carbs: 58 g Fiber: 10 g

Antipasto salad platter

Preparation time: 20 minutes

Cooking time: 0 minute

Servings: 4

Ingredients:

½ chopped red bell pepper

One chopped garlic clove

12 sliced black olive

¼ cup olive oil

2 tbsp balsamic vinegar

1 tbsp chopped basil

Black pepper to taste

6 oz artichoke hearts

5 oz Italian blend

Salt to taste

1 cup broccoli florets

½ cup sliced onion

Eight strawberry tomatoes 3 oz salami dried 4 oz mozzarella cheese

Directions: In a mixing bowl, mix salt, vinegar, olive oil, black pepper, garlic, and basil. The dressing is ready.

Whisk vinaigrette and salad blend in a bowl. Transfer the salad blend mixture to a platter and organize all the leftover ingredients on the platter and serve.

Nutrition Info: Calories: 351 kcal Fat: 25.9 g Protein: 16.2 g Carbs: 14.8 g Fiber: 3.8 g

Greek avocado salad

Preparation time: 20 minutes

Cooking time: 0 minute

Servings: 8

Ingredients:

Two sliced English cucumbers

1.5 lb chopped tomatoes

1/4 sliced red onion 1/2 cups sliced Kalamata olives

1/4 cup chopped parsleysliced avocados

1 cup feta cheese

1/2 cup extra virgin olive oil

1/2 cup red wine vinegar minced garlic cloves

1 tbsp oregano

2 tsp sugar

1 tsp kosher salt

1 tsp ground black pepper

Directions:

Mix tomatoes, parsley, onions, cucumbers, avocado, and olives. Set aside.

Whisk vinegar, sugar, olive oil, salt, oregano, garlic, and pepper in a jar. Close the lid and shake to get the emulsified mixture. You can add salt, black pepper, and sugar to adjust the taste according to you. The dressing is ready.

Transfer the dressing to the salad bowl and toss well. Garnish with feta cheese and serve.

Nutrition Info: Calories: 323 kcal Fat: 29 g Protein: 5 g Carbs: 14 g Fiber: 6 g

One-pan baked halibut and vegetables

Preparation time: 10 minutes

Cooking time: 15 minutes

Servings: 6

Ingredients:

For the Sauce:

Zest of two lemons tsp dried oregano

½ tsp black pepper

1 cup Olive oil

4 tbsp lemon juice

1 tsp seasoned salt tbsp minced garlic tsp dill

¾ tsp coriander

For the Fish

sliced yellow onion

1 lb green beans lb sliced halibut fillet

1 lb cherry tomatoes

Directions: Whisk olive oil, onions, oregano, salt, dill, pepper, tomatoes, lemon zest, green beans, juice, coriander, and garlic in a bowl.

Spread vegetable mixture over one side of the baking tray.

Coat halibut fillets with the sauce and place them on a baking tray.

Pour the leftover sauce over the vegetable mixture and fillets.

Bake in a preheated oven at 425 degrees for 15 minutes.

Nutrition Info: Calories: 390 kcal Fat: 31.3 g Protein: 17.5 g Carbs: 8.8 g Fiber: 4.1 g

Italian baked chicken

Preparation time: 10 minutes

Cooking time: 18 minutes

Servings: 6

Ingredients:

2 lb boneless chicken breast

Pepper to taste tsp thyme

One sliced red onion tsp dry oregano

1 tsp sweet paprika tbsp olive oil minced garlic cloves

1 tbsp of lemon juice halved Campari tomatoes

Salt to taste

Handful chopped parsley for garnishing

Basil leaves as required for garnishing

Directions: Flatten the chicken pieces suing meat mallet in a zip lock bag.

Rub chicken pieces with black pepper and salt and add them to the bowl. Add lemon juice, garlic, oil, and spices and mix well to fully coat the chicken.

Place onions in an oiled baking tray followed by chicken and tomatoes.

Bake in a preheated oven at 425 degrees for 10 minutes while covering the tray with foil.

After ten minutes, uncover and bake again for eight more minutes.

Serve after sprinkle parsley over the baked chicken.

Nutrition Info: Calories: 290 kcal Fat: 11.5 g Protein: 35.9 g Carbs: 11 g Fiber: 0.8 g

Sautéed shrimp and zucchini

Preparation time: 8 minutes

Cooking time: 7 minutes

Servings: 3

Ingredients:

lb shrimp

1 tsp salt

Two zucchinis

2 tbsp chopped garlic

1 tbsp butter

Black pepper to taste

1.5 tbsp lemon juice

2 tbsp chopped parsley

Olive oil as required

Directions :

Add salt, shrimps, and pepper in a bowl. Mix them well.
Cook shrimps in heated oil over medium flame for two minutes from each side.

Shift cooked shrimps in a plate.

Cook zucchini in heated oil in the same pan for two minutes, then sprinkle pepper and salt.

Transfer shrimps to the pan and mix. Add garlic and sauté for two minutes.

Add butter and cook to melt it.

When shrimps, garlic, and zucchini are cooked, add lemon juice and mix well.

Drizzle parsley and serve.

Nutrition Info: Calories: 216 kcal Fat: 6 g Protein: 33 g Carbs: 6 g Fiber: 1 g

Pan-seared citrus shrimp

Preparation time: 5 minutes

Cooking time: 10 minutes

Servings: 6

Ingredients:

1 tbsp olive oil

6 tbsp cup lemon juice

1 cup of orange juice

One sliced orange

Five minced garlic cloves

1 tbsp chopped parsley

1 tbsp chopped red onion

One pinch of red pepper flakes

Kosher salt to taste

Black pepper to taste 3 lb shrimp

One wedge cut lemon

Directions :

Mix parsley, pepper flakes, orange juice, oil, garlic, lemon juice, and onions in a bowl. Transfer the onion mixture to skillet and cook over medium flame for eight minutes.

Add salt, pepper, and shrimps in a skillet and cook for five minutes or until shrimps are done.

Garnish with parsley and lemon slices and serve.

Nutrition Info: Calories: 291 kcal Fat: 6 g Protein: 47 g Carbs: 11 g Fiber: 1 g

Italian roasted vegetables

Preparation time: 10 minutes

Cooking time: 30 minutes

Servings: 6

Ingredients:

8 oz mushrooms

12 oz Campari tomatoes

Extra virgin olive as required

Two sliced zucchinis

12 oz sliced baby potatoes

11 chopped garlic cloves

1 tsp dried thyme

Salt to taste

Shredded Parmesan cheese

Black pepper to taste

½ tbsp dried oregano

Red pepper flakes to taste

Directions :

Add salt, mushrooms, olive oil, pepper, veggies, oregano, garlic, and thyme in a mixing bowl and toss well. Set aside.

Roast potatoes in a preheated oven at 425 degrees for 10 minutes.

Mix the mushroom mixture with baked potatoes and bake for another 20 minutes.

Garnish with cheese and pepper flakes and serve.

Nutrition Info: Calories: 88 kcal Fat: 1 g Protein: 3.8 g Carbs: 14.3 g Fiber: 3.1 g

White bean salad

Preparation time: 15 minutes

Cooking time: 0 minute

Servings: 4

Ingredients:

2o oz white beans

10 oz halved cherry tomatoes

One chopped English cucumber

Four chopped onion

18 chopped mint leaves

1 cup chopped parsley

1 tbsp of lemon juice

Salt to taste

Zested of one lemon

Black pepper to taste

½ tsp Sumac

Feta cheese

1 tsp Za'atar

½ tsp Aleppo

Olive oil

Directions :

Combine all the ingredients in a large salad bowl and toss well to mix everything evenly. Serve and enjoy it.

Nutrition Info: Calories: 310 kcal Fat: 7 g Protein: 16 g Carbs: 47 g Fiber: 11 g

Baked zucchini with thyme and parmesan

Preparation time: 10 minutes

Cooking time: 20 minutes

Servings: 4

Ingredients:

Four sliced zucchinis

1/2 tsp dried thyme

1/2 cup shredded Parmesan cheese

1/2 tsp dried oregano

2 tbsp olive oil

1/4 tsp garlic powder

Kosher salt to taste

1/2 tsp dried basil

Black pepper to taste

2 tbsp chopped parsley

Directions :

Mix all the ingredients in a large bowl except zucchini.

Make a layer of zucchini over a baking sheet sprayed with oil.

Transfer the cheese mixture over zucchini and pour olive oil over them.

Bake in a preheated oven at 350 degrees for 15 minutes, followed by broiling for three minutes. Serve and enjoy it.

Nutrition Info: Calories: 151.3 kcal Fat: 11.2 g Protein: 7.4 g Carbs: 6.8 g Fiber: 2 g

Mediterranean farfalle

Preparation time: 10 minutes

Cooking time: 15 minutes

Servings: 7

Ingredients:

12 oz farfalle pasta

½ cup olive oil

¼ cup chopped basil leaves

1 lb crumbled chorizo sausage

½ cup pine nuts

½ cup shredded parmesan cheese

Two chopped garlic cloves

1 cup diced tomato

¼ cup red wine vinegar

Directions :

In a saucepan, boil water with added salt.

Add pasta and cook until pasta is done.

In a pan, cook chorizo over medium flame. Stir in nuts and cook for five minutes.

Mix garlic and cook for a minute before removing the pan from the flame.

Transfer cooked pasta, vinegar, cheese, cooked chorizo mixture, olive oil, tomatoes, and basil. Mix well to coat everything and serve.

Nutrition Info: Calories: 692 kcal Fat: 48 g Protein: 26.9 g Carbs: 39.7 g Fiber: 15 g

Italian chicken wrap

Preparation time: 10 minutes

Cooking time: 20 minutes

Servings: 4

Ingredients:

2 tbsp butter

1/ 2 cup mayonnaise

1/ 2 lb boneless chicken breasts

1/ 4 cup shredded Parmesan cheese

2 cups shredded romaine lettuce

Four flour tortillas

Two sliced Roma tomatoes

1/ 2 cup crushed croutons

16 basil leaves

Directions : Cook chicken over medium flame in melted butter for 20 minutes. Slice the chicken into strips. Whisk cheese and mayonnaise and pour over the tortilla. Place lettuce followed by chicken, basil, tomato, and croutons on tortilla and wrap. Serve and enjoy it.

Nutrition Info: Calories: 610 kcal Fat: 36 g Protein: 27 g Carbs: 42 g Fiber: 3 g

Orange and berry self-saucing pudding

Preparation time: 10 minutes

Cooking time: 10 minutes

Servings: 04

Ingredients:

125 g berries

Oil spray

½ cup flour

30 g Reduced fat oil

1/4 cup Skim milk

1/4 cup Brown sugar

½ tsp Orange rind

1/4 cup Orange juice

Directions :

Spray oil in four 0.75 -cup microwave-safe trays with oil. Distribute 1/2the berries in 4 dishes.

Put spread in a medium microwave-safe till it is melted. Add flour and milk to melted spread while stirring. Add rind & 1/2 the sugar and mix it well. Fold it in the leftover berries and dress with remaining sugar.

Add juice and 1/3 cup (80ml) boiling water in a jug. Slowly pour the juice into the dishes. Microwave it on (75% power) for 5–6 min. Set down for 5 minutes before serving.

Nutrition Info: Calories: 280 kcal Fat:8 g Protein:5 g Carbs: 44 g Fiber: 3.7g

Cicoria e Fagioli

Preparation time: minutes

Cooking time: minutes

Servings: 6

Ingredients:

- 200 g dried cannellini beans
- 6 tbsp olive oil
- 400 g curly endive
- Four garlic cloves
- 600 ml of water
- Two red chilies
- Salt and pepper to taste

Directions :

Put the dried beans to soak for 12 h (they increase in size). Drain them and boil for two h in fresh unsalted water. Salt at the end of the cooking time. If using canned beans, drain them from their liquid and rinse them before use. Rinse the endive and cut it up into short lengths.

Heat the olive oil, fry the garlic without browning, and then add the endive and chilies. Keeping the heat high, stir-fry for a minute or two, coating the endive with the oil, then add the drained cannellini beans, some salt, and the water. Bring to the boil, cover the pan, and lower the heat. Cook until the endive is soft and most of the liquid has been absorbed.

Nutrition Info: Calories:225 kcal Fat: 21 g Protein: 3 g Carbs: 6 g Fiber:1 g

Eggs Florentine

Preparation time: 10 minutes

Cooking time: 10 minutes

Servings: 3

Ingredients:

- 2 tbsp butter
- Two cloves garlic
- 3 tbsp cream cheese
- ½ cup mushroom
- ½ fresh spinach
- Salt to taste
- Six eggs
- Black pepper to taste

Directions :

Put the butter in a non-stick skillet; heat and mix the mushrooms and garlic till the garlic is flavorsome for about 1 min.

Add spinach to the mushroom paste and cook until spinach is softened for 2 - 3 mins.

Mix the mushroom-spinach mixer; add salt and pepper. Cook, with mixing, until the eggs are stiff; turn.

Pour with cream cheese over the egg mixture and cook before cream cheese started melting just over five minutes.

Nutrition Info: Calories: 278.9 kcal Fat: 22.9 g Protein:15.7 g Carbs: 4.1 g Fiber:22.9

Paleo Baked Eggs in Avocado

Preparation time: 10 minutes

Cooking time: 15 minutes

Servings: 2

Ingredients:
- One pinch parsley
- Two eggs
- Two slice bacon
- One avocado
- 2 tsp chives
- One pinch of salt and black pepper

Directions :

Preheat the oven to 425 degrees.

Break the eggs in a tub, willing to maintain the yolks preserved.

Assemble the avocado halves in the baking bowl, rest them on the side. Slowly spoon one egg yolk in the avocado opening. Keep spooning the white egg into the hole till it is finished. Do the same with leftover egg yolk, egg white, and avocado. Dress with chives, parsley, sea salt, and pepper for each of the avocados.

Gently put the baking dish in the preheated oven and cook for about 15 min well before the eggs are cooked. Sprinkle with bacon over the avocado.

Nutrition Info: Calories: 280.3 kcal Fat:23.5 g Protein: 11.3 g Carbs:9.3 g Fiber:6.9 g

Socca (Farinata)

Preparation time: 10 minutes

Cooking time: 20 minutes

Servings: 4

Ingredients:
- 1 cup chickpea flour
- One pinch salt
- ½ tsp cumin
- Black pepper
- 1 tbsp olive oil
- 1 cup of water
- 1 tbsp vegetable oil

Directions :

In a cup, add chickpea flour, water, and olive oil. Season with salt, cumin, and pepper. Mix all ingredients. Set down at room temperature for two h. Preheat the oven to 450 degrees (230 degrees C). Place a cast-iron skillet in the oven until hot, 5 to 7 minutes. Gently remove the pan from the oven, brush the oil, and pour half of the mixture into the pan, tilting to ensure that it is evenly spread.

Bake in a preheated oven bake it for 7 min. Switch the oven on and let it brown for 1 min. Turn off the oven and shift it to a plate. Do the same with the remaining mixture.

Nutrition Info: Calories: 145.6 kcal Fat: 8.4 g Protein: 4.7 g Carbs:13.8 g Fiber: 0.9 g

Kale and Goat Cheese Frittata Cup

Preparation time: 15 minutes

Cooking time: 15 minutes

Servings: 8

Ingredients:

2 cup kale

3 tbsp olive oil

1/2 tsp dried thyme

One clove garlic

1/4 tsp red pepper

1/4 tsp salt

1/4 cup Goat Cheese

Eight eggs

Black pepper

Directions :

Preheat the oven to 350 F.

Sauté the garlic in 1 tbsp of oil over medium-high heat, in a non-stick skillet, for 30 sec. Add the red pepper flakes and kale to it. Cook for a few minutes until the kale is soft.

Whisk the eggs with pepper and salt in a medium bowl. Add the cooked kale and thyme to it.

Take a muffin tin and brush 8 cups with the remaining oil. Put the mixture in it, topping with goat cheese. Put in the preheated oven and bake for about 30 min. Serve hot.

Nutrition Info: Calories: 110 kcal Fat: 8 g Protein: 8 g Carbs: 3 g Fiber: 1 g

Turkish menemen recipe

Preparation time: 5 minutes

Cooking time: 20 minutes

Servings: 3

Ingredients:

3 tbsp olive oil

4 cup tomatoes

1/4 tsp black pepper

Three green peppers

Four cloves garlic

1/2 tsp salt

Three green onions

Six eggs

Directions :

Heat olive oil in a pan, preferably cast iron. Add the chopped onion and green peppers and sauté until tender.

Add the tomatoes, garlic, and green onions and boil for 10-15 minutes, stirring regularly until cooked down. Sprinkle salt over it.

Let it boil uncovered until the eggs are gently boiled for 8-10 minutes. Enable the egg whites to cook well with a spoon. If you like hard yolks, cook longer.

Dress ground black pepper over it.

Garnish with chopped green onion and mint leaves.

Serve in the pan.

Nutrition Info: Calories:219 kcal Fat:13 g Protein:9 g Carbs: 19.3 g Fiber: 1 g

Almond crusted rack of lamb with rosemary

Preparation time:15 minutes

Cooking time: 15minutes

Servings:

Ingredients:

1.5 kg Racks of Lamb

½ Cup Blanched Almonds

1 tsp of Mint

1 tbsp Dijon Mustard

Pepper to Taste

1 tbsp thyme

Six chopped Rosemary Sprigs

1 tbsp Lemon Juice

2 tbsp Ghee

2 Cloves Garlic

Salt to taste

Directions :

Blend all the items in the blender except lamb.

Sauté lamb in heated oil for two minutes from each side. Set aside.

Coat lamb with mixture and bake in preheated oven for 40 minutes.

Nutrition Info: Calories: 833kcal Fat:40.2 g Protein: 108.3g Carbs: 4.4g Fiber: 2.3g

Citrus orzo salad

Preparation time: 10 minutes

Cooking time: 0 minute

Servings: 3

Ingredients:

Dressing

¼ cup Olive oil

Juice of a half lemon

Juice & zest of half lime

2 tbsp of grated Parmesan cheese

2 tbsp of fresh chopped oregano

¼ tsp flakes of red pepper

Salad

3 cups cooked orzo pasta

One diced yellow bell pepper.

One diced red bell pepper

half chopped small red onion.

One diced medium-sized zucchini

Directions :

Whisk together the olive oil, lemon juice, lime zest, Parmesan lime juice, cheese, red pepper & oregano, flakes in a large bowl & Set aside.

Toss together the orzo, onion, yellow bell pepper, zucchini, and red bell pepper in a bowl.

Now toss well to combine along with dressing & serve.

Nutrition Info: Calories: 474 kcal Fat: 30 g Protein: 10 g Carbs: 42 g Fiber: 4 g ù

Zucchini salad with pomegranate dressing

Preparation time: 8 minutes

Cooking time: 15 minutes

Servings: 6

Ingredients:

One bunch of chives

One pomegranate

1 tbsp pomegranate molasses

1/2 orange juice

1/4 cup mint leaf

120 g feta cheese

2 Lebanese cucumbers

2 tbsp currants

2 tbsp olive oil

Three zucchinis

salt and pepper

Directions :

Clean the zucchini, then cucumber and slice the cucumber and cut it into ribbons using a peeler. And the same thing about your zucchini. Put the cucumber in the fridge.

Chop chives into 2cm chunks and chop mint loosely. Make an orange Juice and combine with olive oil, a touch of pepper and salt, and 1 tbsp of pomegranate molasses to make the dressing. Whisk to blend.

Toss the cucumber and zucchini into the dressing and apply the sliced herbs to prepare the salad. Add flowers and finish with the crumbled feta cheese.

Slice the pomegranate into half and touch the skin's back with the dessert spoon to scatter the seeds over the salad.

Nutrition Info: Calories: 177.7 kcal Fat: 9.8 g Protein: 5.7 g Carbs: 20 g Fiber: 3.9 g

Pomegranate Molasses Chicken with Bulgur Salad

Preparation time: 15 minutes

Cooking time: 15 minutes

Servings: 4

Ingredients:

One tablespoon vegetable oil

¼ cup pomegranate seeds

1/3 cup chopped, roasted pistachios, unsalted

½ cup mint chopped

½ cup dried currants

¾ cup chopped parsley

1 cup quick-cooking bulgur

One serrano Chile, thinly sliced

Two garlic cloves, thinly sliced

2 pounds skinless, boneless chicken thighs

Two tablespoons olive oil

Four tablespoons pomegranate molasses*, divided

Kosher salt and freshly ground black pepper

Directions :

Put 3 tbsp ginger, chili peppers in the chicken.

A medium bowl of pomegranate molasses; season with pepper and salt. Cover and leave for a minimum of 2 hours to relax.

Cook bulgur as per box instructions. On a baking sheet, drain and spread out, let cool.

Combine the bulgur, currants, olive oil, pistachios, 3/4 cup of parsley, 1/2 cup of mint, and 1 tbsp. Stir in a big bowl of pomegranate molasses; season with pepper and salt.

Heat the oil in a big, medium skillet. Take chicken from the marinade and cook till golden brown, operating in 2 batches, around 4 minutes each side (turn down the heat if necessary).

Nutrition Info: Calories: 521 kcal Fat: 20 g Protein: 25 g Carbs: 63 g Fiber: 9 g

Creamy and rich Spicy Pumpkin

Preparation time: 5 minutes

Cooking time: 25 minutes

Servings: ¼

Ingredients:

1 cup milk

15 oz pumpkin puree

One clove garlic, minced

One onion, chopped

1/2 tsp Cajun seasoning

1/4 tbsp heavy cream

1/4 tsp crushed red pepper

2 1/2 cups chicken broth

2 tbsp brown sugar

2 tbsp butter

Pepitas, for serving

Pinch of cayenne pepper

Directions :

Over the medium-high heat, heat the butter in the big saucepan either in a Dutch oven. Add the onion and simmer for about 4 minutes, constantly stirring, until tender. Apply the garlic and then cook for an extra thirty seconds. Apply the Cajun, cayenne pepper, and red pepper. Season and steam for another 30 seconds. Add a pumpkin puree and broth with the chicken. Until smooth, stir. Bring to boil, then simmer for 10-15 mins and reduce the heat. Move the soup to a mixer or food processor, in batches. Tightly cover and mix until smooth. Set the soup back in the dish. Add brown sugar and whisk until melted, when the heat is low. Add in the milk gently, and stir constantly. Taste, then change the taste of the seasonings. If required, finish each serving with tablespoons of cream and pepitas.

Nutrition Info: Calories: 168 kcal Fat: 7 g Protein: 6 g Carbs: 16 g Fiber: 1 g

Chickpea & Pomegranate Dip

Preparation time: 10 minutes

Cooking time: 0 minute

Servings: 5

Ingredients:

3 tbsp pomegranate molasses

2 tbsp chopped mint

2 tbsp chopped coriander

12 oz chickpeas

1/4 cup minced red Onion

1/4 cup crumbled feta cheese

1/2 tsp salt

1/2 tsp hot pepper flakes

1/2 cup olive oil

One clove garlic minced

1 tsp ground cumin

Directions :

Put pulse chickpeas, pomegranate molasses, oil, all but one teaspoon (about 5 mL) both of the mint & coriander along with cumin, salt, and pepper flakes together in the food processor until mixed, but still a little bit chunky.

Onion pulse; whisk in garlic. Scrap the serving bowl into it. (Make-ahead: Up to 24 hours to cover and refrigerate.) Dust with feta and leftover mint and coriander.

Nutrition Info: Calories: 62 kcal Fat: 3 g Protein: 1 g Carbs: 6 g Fiber: 1 g

Herb-Baked Fish Fillets

Preparation time: 15 minutes

Cooking time: 15 minutes

Servings: 4

Ingredients:

Kosher salt to taste

Black pepper to taste

2 tbsp butter

1/4 tsp dried thyme

1/4 cup corn flakes

1/4 cup chopped Onion

1/2 tsp dried tarragon

1 tsp chopped parsley

1 tbsp melted butter

1 lb fish fillets

One clove garlic (minced)

Directions :

Sauté garlic, onions, thyme, and tarragon in heated butter for two minutes.

Transfer the mixture over fish fillets.

Lightly sauté corn in butter and sprinkle salt and pepper to make cornflake crumbs.

Bake the fillets in a preheated oven at 450 degrees for 15 minutes.

Serve and enjoy it.

Nutrition Info: Calories: 225 kcal Fat: 7 g Protein: 9 g Carbs: 34 g Fiber: 8 g

Vegetarian three-cheese quiche stuffed pepper

Preparation time: 5 minutes

Cooking time: 55 minutes

Servings: 2

Ingredients:

1/2 cup Parmesan Cheese

2 Bell Peppers

1/2 cup Grated Mozzarella Cheese

4 Egg

1/2 cup Ricotta Cheese

1 tsp Garlic Powder

1/4 tsp Parsley

1/4 cup Spinach

2 tbsp Parmesan Cheese

Directions :

Heat the oven to 375 degrees.

Prepare peppers by slicing them in 4 equal halves & removing seeds

Take food processor & blend cheese, garlic powder, parsley & eggs.

Pour the mixture of egg into the pepper.

Place some spinach leaves on the top & stir with a fork.

Cover with the foil & bake 35-45 min.

Sprinkle Parmesan cheese & broil 3-5 min.

Nutrition Info: Calories: 245.5 kcal Fat: 16.3 g
Protein: 17.8 g Carbs: 6 g Fiber: 2.1 g

Cauliflower hash brown breakfast bowl

Preparation time: 5 minutes

Cooking time: 10 minutes

Servings: 6

Ingredients:

2 cups shredded cauliflower

1/4 tsp garlic powder

1 tbsp olive oil

1/2 tsp salt

Two eggs

1/3 cup green onions

1/4 tsp black pepper

Directions :

Grate cauliflower head on a cheese grater.

Take a mixing bowl and combine cauliflower with the eggs, onion, salt, black pepper, & garlic powder.

Stir it to mix well. Heat olive oil in a skillet.

Add cauliflower mixture to pan & press with a spatula.

Cook for 2-3 min.

Carefully flip & cook for 2-3 min to let edges brown.

Form a circular shape with the help of a spatula.

Repeat the same process with remaining.

Garnish the dish with onion serves hot.

Nutrition Info: Calories: 61 kcal Fat: 3 g Protein: 4 g Carbs: 5 g Fiber: 2 g

Carrot salad

Preparation time: 20 minutes

Cooking time: 0 minute

Servings: 4

Ingredients:

1 lb carrots

2 tbsp green onion

2 tbsp parsley

Dressing

2 tbsp olive oil

1/4 tsp sea salt

2 tbsp lemon juice

1 tsp Dijon mustard

2 tsp honey

1/2 tsp cumin

Directions :

Take 3 cups of grated carrots & place in a bowl.

Now add parsley & chickpea (optional)

For the dressing, whisk all ingredients together in a bowl till they are completely blended.

Now pour dressing on the carrot mixture & continue stirring till the mixture is coated evenly.

For a mind-blowing taste, let the salad marinate for twenty minutes & toss before serving.

Nutrition Info: Calories: 210 kcal Fat: 8.9 g Protein: 5.7 g Carbs: 29.1 g Fiber: 7.3 g

Fruity asparagus quinoa salad

Preparation time: 15 minutes

Cooking time: 5 minutes

Servings: 7

Ingredients:

2 cups cooked quinoa

3 tsp olive oil

30 sliced spears asparagus

1/2 tsp salt

1/4 tsp pepper

Two cloves garlic

Salt and pepper

16 sliced strawberries

4.5 oz mozzarella cheese

1/3 cup Balsamic Vinaigrette

2 tbsp basil

Directions :

Place cooked quinoa in a bowl.

Prepare the balsamic vinaigrette & set aside.

Heat olive oil in a pan to overheat.

Once heated, add asparagus & garlic.

Sprinkle with salt & pepper. Cook 2-3 min.

Add asparagus to quinoa.

Mix the strawberries, balsamic vinaigrette & cheese.

Toss to mix well. Top salad with the basil.

Nutrition Info: Calories: 178 kcal Fat: 5.5 g Protein: 10.3 g Carbs: 21.1 g Fiber: 4.6 g

Broccoli and Tomato Pasta

Preparation time: 20 minutes

Cooking time: 20 minutes

Servings: 4

Ingredients:

3 quarts' water

8 oz spaghetti

2 cups broccoli

Two tomatoes chopped

Two minced garlic cloves

1/2 tsp red pepper

2 tbsp olive oil

1/4 cup Romano cheese grated

1/2 cup olives sliced

1/2 cup minced parsley

3/4 tsp salt

1/8 tsp pepper

Directions :

Boil water in a pan, add spaghetti, and boil for 5 minutes. Transfer broccoli and boil for 3 to 4 minutes until pasta & broccoli gets tender. In a nonstick skillet, sauté tomatoes, garlic & pepper flakes, 2 minutes.

Drain the pasta mixture, and add to skillet. Now add remaining ingredients & toss to coat. Serve.

Nutrition Info: Calories: 348 kcal Fat:12 g Protein: 12 g Carbs: 51 g Fiber: 5 g

Black Eyed Peas

Preparation time: 2 minutes

Cooking time: 80 minutes

Servings: 12

Ingredients:

2 cups dried Black-eyed peas

Five cloves chopped Garlic

12 oz Smoked turkey

3 ½ cups Water

One chopped Onion

one pinch Cayenne pepper

1/2 tsp Ginger

One cup diced Celery

1/2 tsp thyme

1/2 tsp Curry powder

Directions :

Take a large bowl. Add black-eyed peas. Pour water over them (just enough to cover the peas by about 4 inches). Cover the bowl and let soak overnight (or at least six hours).

Rinse the peas under cold water; Drain. Take a large pot; add all the remaining ingredients and black-eyed peas to the pot. Bring to boil. After the first boil, reduce heat to low.

Cook until peas are tender (covered with a lid) for about 1 hour.

Stir occasionally.

Nutrition Info: Calories: 304 kcal Fat: 24 g Protein: 12 g Carbs: 8 g Fiber: 1 g

Simple tuna pasta

Preparation time: 5 minutes

Cooking time: 10 minutes

Servings: 2

Ingredients:

2 tbsp olive oil

Two minced cloves garlic

5 oz tuna

1 tsp lemon juice

1 tbsp chopped parsley

Salt to taste

Black pepper to taste

4 oz uncooked pasta

Directions : Cook pasta accordingly in boiling water for seven minutes. Sauté garlic in heated oil for half a minute over medium flame. Add tuna, parsley, and lemon juice. Cook for another minute. Add three spoons of pasta water and mix well. Mix drained pasta and toss well.

Nutrition Info: Calories: 400 kcal Fat: 16 g Protein: 21 g Carbs: 44 g Fiber: 2 g

Lebanese rice with vermicelli

Preparation time: 15 minutes

Cooking time: 20 minutes

Servings: 6

Ingredients:

Salt to taste

2 cups long-grain rice

1 cup broken vermicelli

Water

2.5 tbsp olive oil

½ cup toasted pine nuts

Directions :

Soak rice in water for 30 minutes. Cook vermicelli in heated olive oil over a high flame until it turned brown. Mix drained rice and mix. Sprinkle salt and continue stirring to mix them well.

Add water and boil it to concentrate the mixture. Reduce the heat, cover, and cook for 21 minutes over low flame. Serve and enjoy it.

Nutrition Info: Calories: 309 kcal Fat: 8.3 g Protein: 5.6 g Carbs: 51.5 g Fiber: 1.5 g

Crepes with passion fruit

Preparation time: 5 minutes

Cooking time: 10 minutes

Servings: 4

Ingredients:

Crepes

Two eggs

1/25 cups oat milk

1 cup flour

1/5 tbsp butter

Sauce

½ cup of sugar

¾ cup of passion fruit

Directions :

Mix eggs, milk, and flour and keep it aside. Mix sugar with passion fruit and boil it to reduce the concentration to half. Melt the butter and spread crepe mixture in a pan and cook for 2 minutes from both sides. Transfer the crepe to a plate with sauce and serve.

Nutrition Info: Calories: 280 kcal Fat: 15.5 g Protein: 1 g Carbs: 2 g Fiber: 0 g

Chocolate Crunch Cookies

Preparation Time: 15 Minutes

Cooking Time: 10 Minutes

Serving: 35 cookies

Ingredients

1 1/2 cups chocolate chips

1.5 cups butter

Two eggs

One tsp baking soda

2 cups of sugar

One tsp vanilla

One tsp salt

1/2 cup pecans

2 cups oats

2 cups flour

2 cups Krispies Rice

Directions :

Whisk all the ingredients in a large mixing bowl and pour the batter into a baking tray. Bake in a preheated oven at 350 degrees for ten minutes.

Nutrition Info: Calories: 271 kcal Fat: 14 g Protein: 48 g Carbs: 35 g Fiber: 0.1 g

Authentic Turkey Kebabs

Servings: 6

Cooking Time: 30 Minutes

Ingredients:

1 ½ pounds turkey breast, cubed

3 Spanish peppers, sliced

2 zucchinis, cut into thick slices

1 onion, cut into wedges

2 tablespoons olive oil, room temperature

1 tablespoon dry ranch seasoning

Directions:

Thread the turkey pieces and vegetables onto bamboo skewers. Sprinkle the skewers with dry ranch seasoning and olive oil.

Grill your kebabs for about 10 minutes, turning them periodically to ensure even cooking.

Storing

Wrap your kebabs in foil before packing them into airtight containers; keep in your refrigerator for up to 3 to days.

For freezing, place your kebabs in airtight containers or heavy-duty freezer bags. Freeze up to 2-3 months. Defrost in the refrigerator. Bon appétit!

Nutrition Info: 2 Calories; 13.8g Fat; 6.7g Carbs; 25.8g Protein; 1.2g Fiber

Rainbow Salad With Roasted Chickpeas

Servings: 2-3

Cooking Time: 40 Minutes

Ingredients:

Creamy avocado dressing, store bought or homemade

3 large tri-color carrots - one orange, one red, and one yellow

1 medium zucchini

1/4 cup fresh basil, cut into ribbons

1 can chickpeas, rinsed and drained

1 tbsp olive oil

1 tsp chili powder

1/2 tsp cumin

Salt, to taste

Pepper, to taste

Directions:

Preheat the oven to 400 degrees F

Pat the chickpeas dry with paper towels

Add them to a bowl and toss with the olive oil, chili powder, cumin, and salt and pepper

Arrange the chickpeas on a baking sheet in a single layer

Bake for 30-40 minutes - making sure to shaking the pan once in a while to prevent over browning. The chickpeas will be done when they're crispy and golden brown, allow to cool

With a grater, peeler, mandolin or spiralizer, shred the carrots and zucchini into very thin ribbons

Once the zucchini is shredded, lightly press it with paper towels to remove excess moisture

Add the shredded zucchini and carrots to a bowl, toss with the basil

Add in the roasted chickpeas, too gently to combine

Distribute among the containers, store for 2 days

To Serve: Top with the avocado dressing and enjoy

Nutrition Info: (without dressing): Calories:640;Total Fat: 51g;Total Carbs: 9.8g;Protein: 38.8g

Sour And Sweet Fish

Servings: 2

Cooking Time: 25 Minutes

Ingredients:

1 tablespoon vinegar

2 drops stevia

1 pound fish chunks

¼ cup butter, melted

Salt and black pepper, to taste

Directions:

Put butter and fish chunks in a skillet and cook for about 3 minutes.

Add stevia, salt and black pepper and cook for about 10 minutes, stirring continuously.

Dish out in a bowl and serve immediately.

Place fish in a dish and set aside to cool for meal prepping. Divide it in 2 containers and refrigerate for up to 2 days. Reheat in microwave before serving.

Nutrition Info: Calories: 2 ;Carbohydrates: 2.8g;Protein: 24.5g;Fat: 16.7g;Sugar: 2.7g;Sodium: 649mg

Papaya Mangetout Stew

Servings: 2

Cooking Time: 5 Minutes

Ingredients:

2 cups Mangetout

2 cups bean sprouts

1 tablespoon water

1 papaya, peeled, deseeded, and cubed

1 lime, juiced

2 tablespoon unsalted peanuts

small handful basil leaves, torn

small handful mint leaves, chopped

Directions:

Take a large frying pan and place it over high heat.

Add Mangetout, 1 tablespoon of water, and bean sprouts.

Cook for about 2-minutes.

Remove from heat, add papaya, and lime juice.

Toss everything well.

Spread over containers.

Before eating, garnish with herbs and peanuts.

Enjoy!

Nutrition Info: Calories: 283, Total Fat: 6.4 g, Saturated Fat: 0.g, Cholesterol: 0 mg, Sodium: 148 mg, Total Carbohydrate: 42.8 g, Dietary Fiber: 4.9 g, Total Sugars: 21.5 g, Protein: 20.1 g, Vitamin D: 0 mcg, Calcium: 205 mg, Iron: 3 mg, Potassium: 743 mg

Salmon With Warm Tomato-olive Salad

Servings: 4

Cooking Time: 25 Minutes

Ingredients:

Salmon fillets (4/approx. 4 oz./1.25-inches thick)

Celery (1 cup)

Medium tomatoes (2)

Fresh mint (.25 cup)

Kalamata olives (.5 cup)

Garlic (.5 tsp.)

Salt (1 tsp. + more to taste)

Honey (1 tbsp.)

Red pepper flakes (.25 tsp.)

Olive oil (2 tbsp. + more for the pan)

Vinegar (1 tsp.)

Directions:

Slice the tomatoes and celery into inch pieces and mince the garlic. Chop the mint and the olives.

Heat the oven using the broiler setting.

Whisk the oil, vinegar, honey, red pepper flakes, and salt (1 tsp.. Brush the mixture onto the salmon.

Line the broiler pan with a sheet of foil. Spritz the pan lightly with olive oil, and add the fillets (skin side downward.

Broil them for four to six minutes until well done.

Meanwhile, make the tomato salad. Mix ½ teaspoon of the salt with the garlic.

Prepare a small saucepan on the stovetop using the med-high temperature setting. Pour in the rest of the oil and add the garlic mixture with the olives and one tablespoon of vinegar. Simmer for about three minutes.

Prepare the serving dishes. Pour the bubbly mixture into the bowl and add the mint, tomato, and celery. Dust it with the salt as desired and toss.

When the salmon is done, serve with a tomato salad.

Nutrition Info: Calories: 433;Protein: 38 grams; Fat: 26 grams